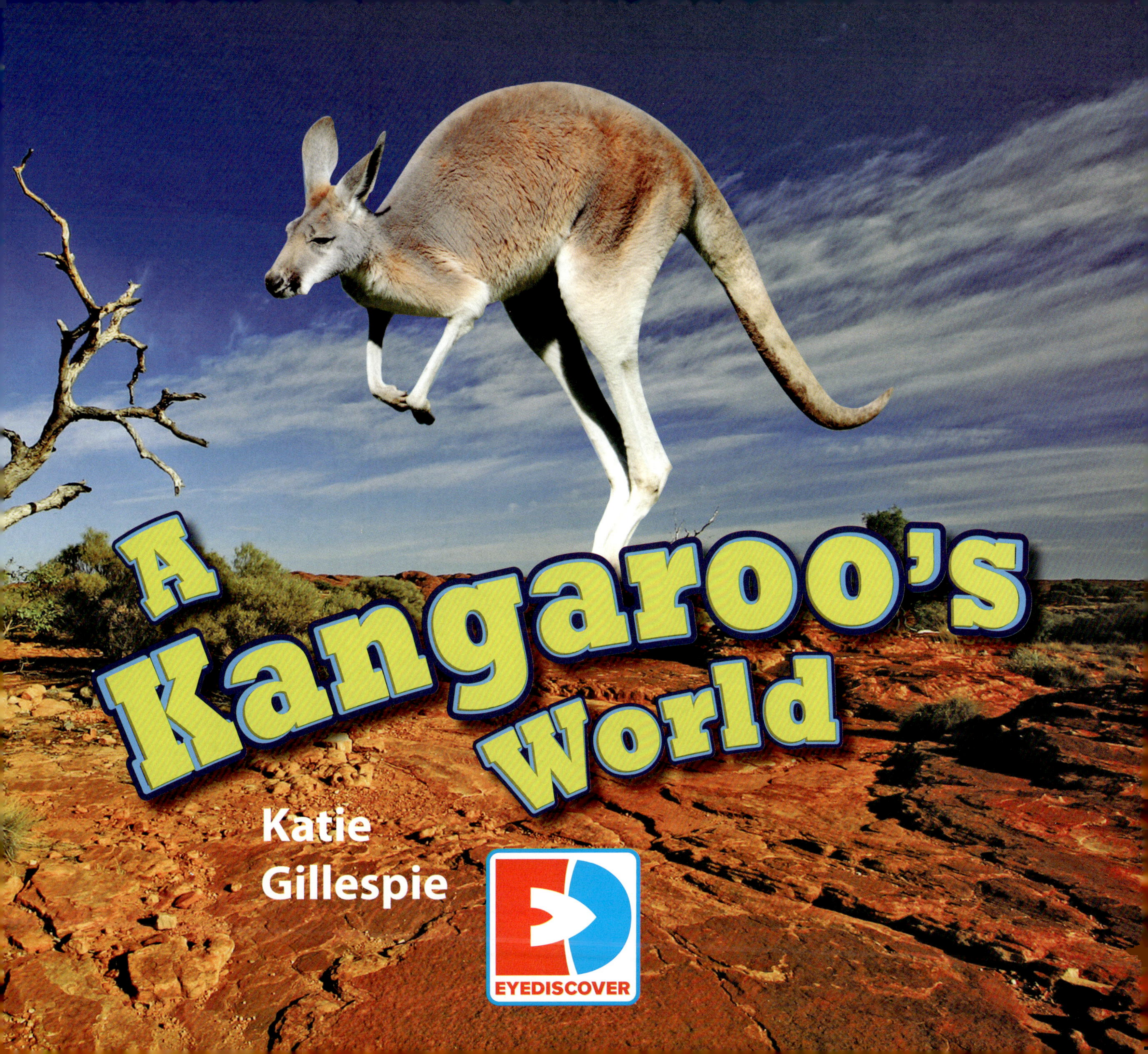
A Kangaroo's World
Katie Gillespie
EYEDISCOVER

Go to **www.eyediscover.com** and enter this book's unique code.

BOOK CODE

S224587

EYEDISCOVER brings you optic readalongs that support active learning.

Published by AV² by Weigl
350 5th Avenue, 59th Floor New York, NY 10118
Website: www.eyediscover.com

Library of Congress Control Number: 2017930716

ISBN 978-1-4896-5668-1 (hardcover)

Printed in the United States of America
in Brainerd, Minnesota
1 2 3 4 5 6 7 8 9 0 21 20 19 18 17

022017
020317

Editor: Katie Gillespie
Designer: Mandy Christiansen

Weigl acknowledges Getty Images and iStock as the primary image suppliers for this title.

EYEDISCOVER provides enriched content, optimized for tablet use, that supplements and complements this book. EYEDISCOVER books strive to create inspired learning and engage young minds in a total learning experience.

Watch
Video content brings each page to life.

Browse
Thumbnails make navigation simple.

Read
Follow along with text on the screen.

Listen
Hear each page read aloud.

Your EYEDISCOVER Optic Readalongs come alive with...

Audio
Listen to the entire book read aloud.

Video
High resolution videos turn each spread into an optic readalong.

OPTIMIZED FOR

- ☑ TABLETS
- ☑ WHITEBOARDS
- ☑ COMPUTERS
- ☑ AND MUCH MORE!

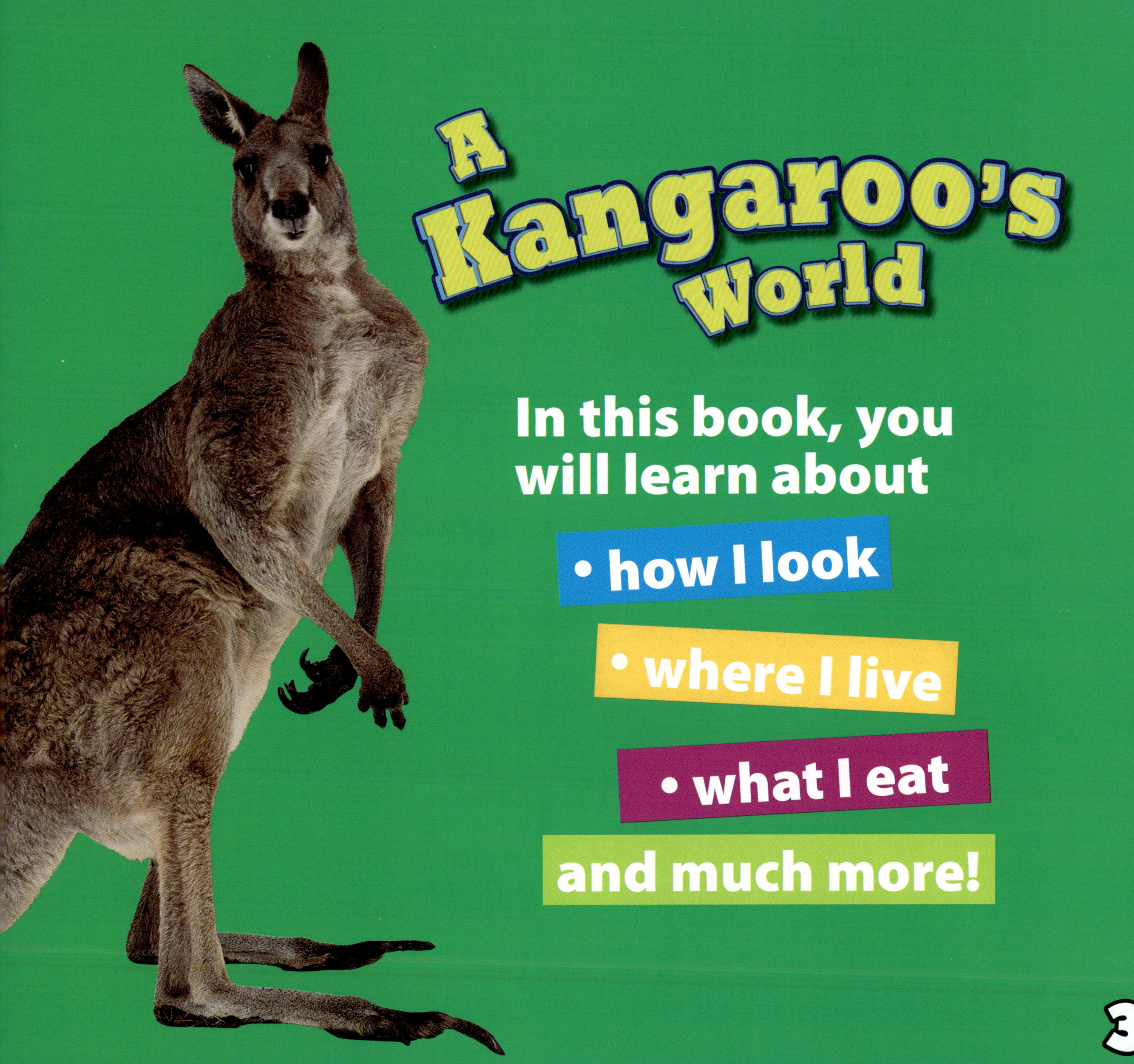

A Kangaroo's World

In this book, you will learn about

- how I look
- where I live
- what I eat

and much more!

I am a kangaroo.

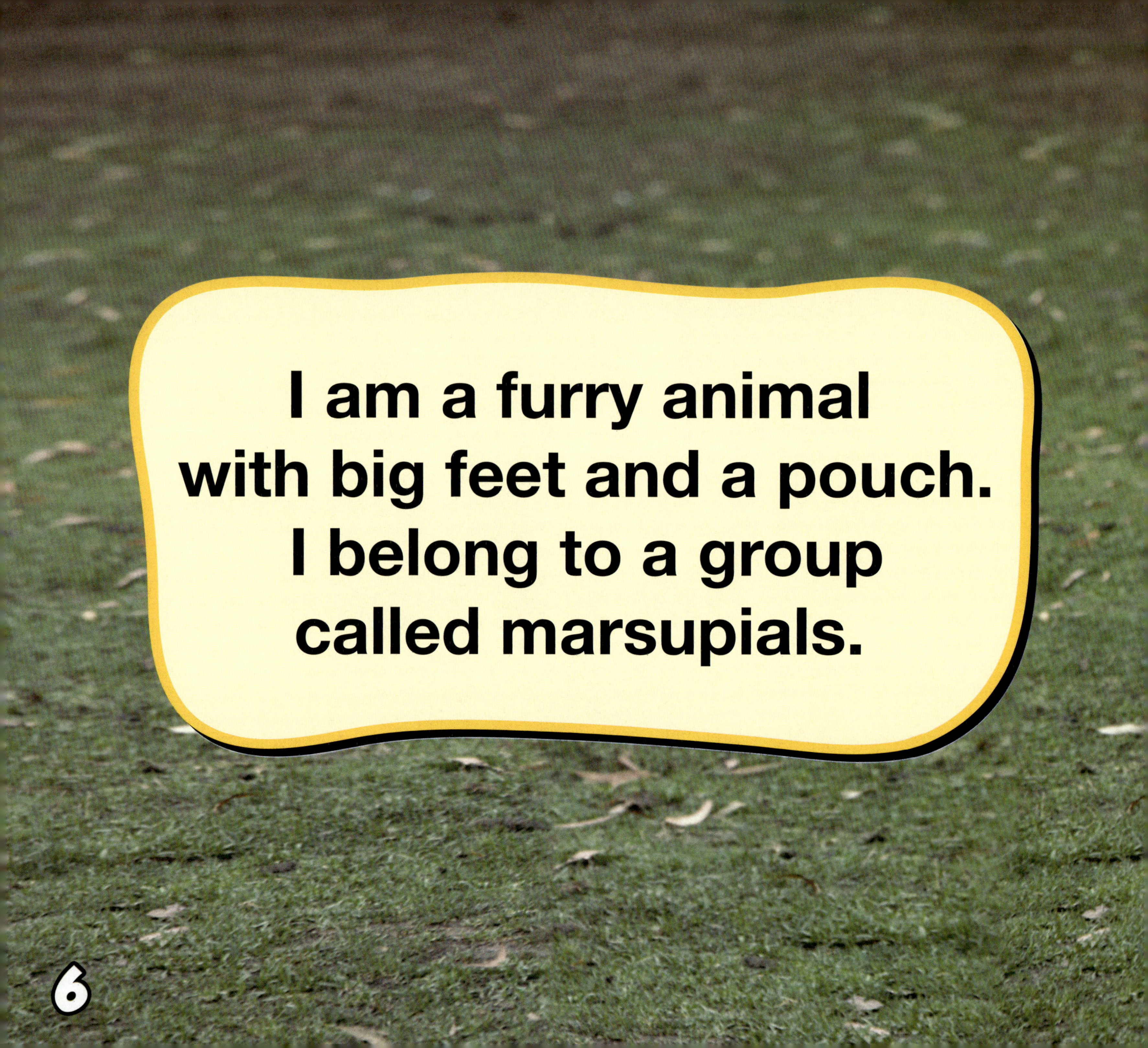

I am a furry animal
with big feet and a pouch.
I belong to a group
called marsupials.

I am found mostly in Australia.

I was called a joey when I was a baby. My mother kept me safe inside her pouch.

My body is built for hopping. My strong back legs act just like springs.

I drank my mother's milk
when I was young.
Now grasses and other plants
are my favorite foods.

My tail is very long. It helps me keep my balance.

I am most active at night.

My powerful legs can kick very hard. If you see me, stay away.

KANGAROOS BY THE NUMBERS

Large kangaroos can **hop at speeds** of **40 miles per hour.** This is about as **fast** as a **horse** can gallop. (64 kilometers per hour)

Some **kangaroos** can **live** for 20 **years or more.**

Joeys **leave** their mother's **pouch** between **7 and 10 months** of age.

There are more than **50 million** kangaroos living in **Australia.**

There are **6 different species** of **kangaroos.**

Newborn kangaroos are only 0.75 inches long.

This is **the size** of a **large bee.** (1.9 centimeters)

KEY WORDS

Research has shown that as much as 65 percent of all written material published in English is made up of 300 words. These 300 words cannot be taught using pictures or learned by sounding them out. They must be recognized by sight. This book contains 43 common sight words to help young readers improve their reading fluency and comprehension. This book also teaches young readers several important content words, such as proper nouns. These words are paired with pictures to aid in learning and improve understanding.

Page	Sight Words First Appearance
4	a, am, I
6	and, animal, big, feet, group, to, with
8	found, in
11	her, me, mother, my, was, when
12	back, for, is, just, like
15	are, foods, now, other, plants, young
16	helps, it, keep, long, very
19	at, most, night
20	away, can, hard, if, see, you

Page	Content Words First Appearance
4	kangaroo
6	marsupials, pouch
8	Australia
11	baby, joey
12	body, legs, springs
15	grasses, milk
16	balance, tail

Watch
Video content brings each page to life.

Browse
Thumbnails make navigation simple.

Read
Follow along with text on the screen.

Listen
Hear each page read aloud.

Go to www.eyediscover.com and enter this book's unique code.

BOOK CODE

S224587